Hide-and-Seek Gorillas

Happy House

About Wise & Wide

- A systematic 6-level English reading program based on Lexile® measures
- Diverse and interesting topics chosen from the elementary curriculums of Korea and English speaking western countries
- Well-written books in various forms including fiction stories, descriptive texts, and classics retold
- The informative but original fiction stories grab your interest, leading to the easy and clear understanding of the educational content.
- Improve thinking skills with solid after-reading activities at all levels of the series.

Wise & Wide is a 6-level English reading program that consists of 60 books and each level is systematically divided by Lexile® measures. The Lexile® Framework for Reading is the most popular reading measuring system in American formal education curriculums and many English programs. Over 20 out of 50 states in the U.S. mark Lexile® measures directly on students' final report cards and over 300 well-known publishers adopt and use Lexile® measures.

Experience many kinds of readings written by professional writers from the U.S. and England. They used interesting topics that were carefully chosen after analyzing elementary curriculums from around the world including Korea, the U.S., England, and Australia among many others. Comprehensive after-reading activities including graphic organizers, speaking tasks, and After-reading Tests are ready for you.

Levels in the series and their corresponding Lexile® measures

Level	Lexile® measures	U.S. Grade
Level 1	Below 200L	Pre K - K
Level 2	190L - 400L	Lower Grade 1
Level 3	350L - 530L	Upper Grade 1
Level 4	420L - 650L	Grade 2
Level 5	520L - 940L	Grade 3 - 4
Level 6	830L - 1070L	Grade 5 - 6

* Smart Readers: Wise & Wide level 1 is applicable to the preschool level in the U.S.
* The source of the relationship between Lexile® measures and U.S. school grades: CCSS(Common Core State Standards) FOR ENGLISH LANGUAGE ARTS, APPENDIX A (2012, which is used by 45 states in the U.S.)

Topic List

	Level 1	Level 2	Level 3	Level 4	Level 5	Level 6
Book 1	Science›Biology: The hibernation of animals Story	Science›Biology: Living and nonliving things Story	Science›Biology› Animals & the Environment: Sea otters Story	Environment› Living with nature: The diver & the persimmon tree Story	Science›Biology› Animal: Amazing animals of the Amazon Story	Science›Biology: Germs, transmitted diseases Story
Book 2	Literature› World classics: Aesop's fables Story	Literature› Traditional fairy tale: Old tales about stones Story	Social Studies› Economy: To run a business to make and save money Story	Science›Biology› Plants: Photosynthesis Story	Science›Earth science: Earth's layers, earthquakes, volcanoes, and earth's atmosphere Report	Mathematics› Sequence: The golden ratio & the Fibonacci sequence Story
Book 3	Science›Physics: How shadows are formed Story	Literature› World classics: Peter Pan Story	Science›Scientific technology: Nanobots Story	Literature›Myths: World's creation stories Story	Literature› Legend: The story of King Arthur Story	Literature›Myths: Constellation myths Story
Book 4	Literature› Traditional literature: The Talmud Story	Science›Biology› Animal: Polar bears Story	Science›Biology› Animal: Mountain gorillas Story	Social Studies› Cultural anthropology: Amazing ancient cultures of the world Story	Science› Earth science: Clouds and weather Story	
Book 5	Social Studies› Ethics: Rules in daily life Story	Science›Biology: The five senses Report	Social Studies› Cultural anthropology: Astonishing festivals Report	Art›Music: Stories from two operas Story	Social Studies› World culture & history: The Renaissance Story	
Book 6	Social Studies› World geography & travel: Tourist attractions around the world Story	Science›Biology› Animal: Dinosaurs Story	Science› Astronomy: The solar system Story	Social Studies› People: Three great people who overcame hardships Story	Science›Scientific technology: The wonderful world of robots Report	
Book 7				Science & Social Studies› Technology & culture: Inventions from around the world Report	Art›Works of art: Famous paintings Report	
Book 8						
Book 9						
Book 10						

* 10 books in each level will be published.

How to Use This Book

•Before Reading

You can easily find the topic and what kind of story you are about to read.

•The text

All the stories were written by professional writers from the U.S. and England, so you will read authentic and appropriate English sentences and expressions in every book in the series.

•Pop Quiz

Check out right away if you understand what you have just read by solving a pop quiz that checks your comprehension.

•Key Words

The key words and expressions on each page are listed for you to easily study them.

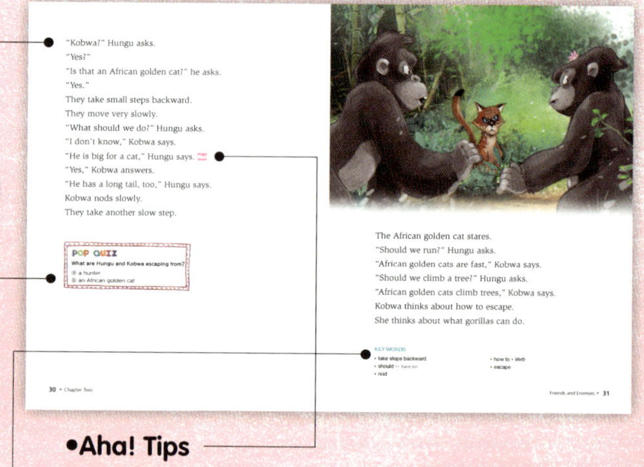

•Aha! Tips

Download free Korean explanations at *www.ihappyhouse.co.kr* for all of the sentences marked with "Aha!". These explain cultural, scientific, and economic knowledge or they deal with aspects of English such as grammatical structures or idiomatic expressions. There are lots of "Aha! Tips" to help you understand the text.

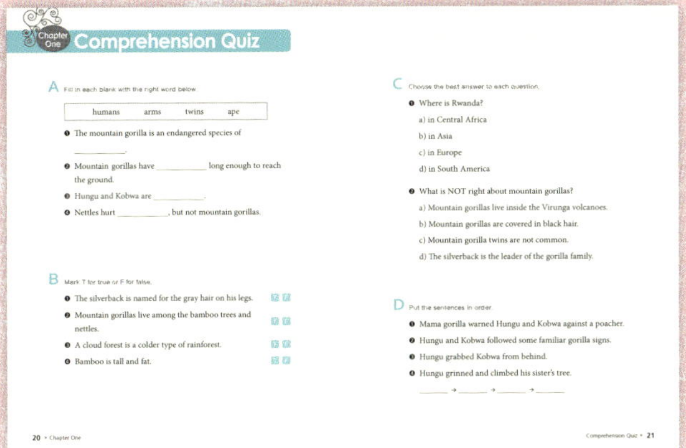

•Comprehension Quiz

After reading one chapter, solve various questions to find out if you fully understand the content.

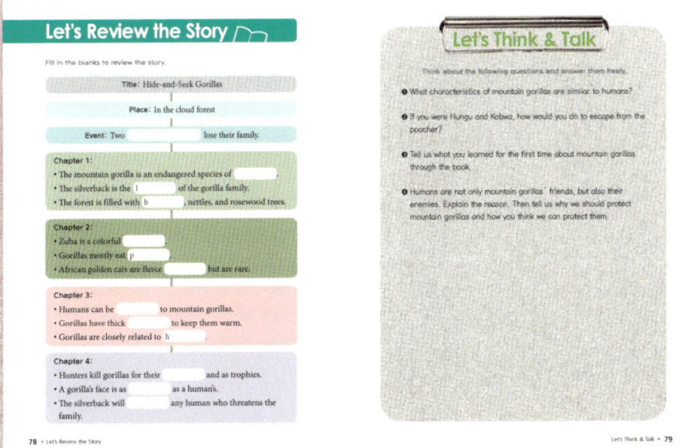

•Let's Review the Story /
•Let's Think & Talk

Fill in the blanks in the organizer to summarize the whole story. Express your own thinking and feelings about the story by answering the questions. You can build up logic and reasoning skills for your essay examinations in the future.

Appendix

Audio CD
In the CD audio book form, the texts are read vividly by American professional voice actors.

After-reading Test
Solve an additionally provided After-reading Test for each book.

The Korean translation, Answer Keys, a Word Quiz, a Word List, and Aha! Tips for each book
You can download them for free at *www.ihappyhouse.co.kr*

Before Reading

Hide-and-Seek Gorillas

Level 3–4,
Lexile® 410L

- Science〉Biology〉Animal
- Story

The main character in movie <King Kong>, mountain gorilla

Like its name, a mountain gorilla is a gorilla that lives on a high mountain. It lives in a mountainous area located at an altitude of 2,300~3,500 meters. Around 350 mountain gorillas live in the Virunga Mountains which are a chain of volcanoes, stretch across Rwanda, the Democratic Republic of the Congo and Uganda in Africa.

Unlike lowland gorillas that we can usually see at the zoo, there are only about 650 mountain gorillas currently all over the world due to loss of habitat, poaching, and civil wars among tribes. So they are animals that need to be protected. Mountain gorillas are led by a male leader, a silverback, and under his leadership, they form their family and live. Unlike their vicious-looking appearance, they usually eat plants. Also, they are genetically over 90% identical to humans, so they are one of the closest animals to humans.

Through the story of Hungu and Kobwa who were separated from their family while playing hide-and-seek, let's find out more about mountain gorillas.

Summary

A mountain gorilla family lives in a forest in the Virunga volcanoes. One day while playing hide-and-seek, mountain gorilla twin siblings, Hungu and Kobwa became separated from their family. Kobwa got nervous because her family had disappeared, but, like any male gorilla that wanted in the future to be a silverback leading a horde of gorillas, Hungu wasn't scared.

Hungu and Kobwa had a thrilling and exciting adventure while looking for their family. When they encountered an African golden cat known to attack young gorillas, they escaped from it with Kobwa's wit. When they encountered tourists tracking mountain gorilla, they had a good time with them. But then someone else appeared. He looked similar to the gorilla tracking guide that they had met before, but he was somewhat different. The stern-looking man was holding something in his hand. Oh my, he was a poacher!

How will Hungu and Kobwa escape this danger?

Contents

Hide-and-Seek Gorillas

2   About Wise & Wide
4   How to Use This Book
6   Before Reading

Chapter One
10   Playing Games
20   Comprehension Quiz

Chapter Two
22   Friends and Enemies
36   Comprehension Quiz

Chapter Three
38   Tourists
56   Comprehension Quiz

Chapter Four
58   Poacher
76   Comprehension Quiz

78   Let's Review the Story
79   Let's Think & Talk
80   Let's Review the Story (Answers)
81   After-reading Test

Hide-and-Seek Gorillas

Playing Games

An amazing creature lives deep in the cloud forest.

It lives in Volcanoes National Park in Rwanda.

Rwanda is a country in Central Africa.

Rwanda is smaller than South Korea.

The amazing creature is the mountain gorilla.

It is an endangered species of ape.

Mountain gorillas only live on the slopes of the Virunga volcanoes.

Most of the volcanoes are dormant.

They are sleeping.

A couple of volcanoes are active.

Sometimes they rumble and spew ash.

A cloud forest is a colder type of rainforest.

A cloud forest grows on mountain slopes.

Humans do not live in the cloud forest.

KEY WORDS

- play game
- amazing
- creature
- cloud forest
- Volcanoes National Park
- Rwanda
- Central Africa
- endangered
- species
- ape
- slope
- dormant
- a couple of
- active
- rumble
- spew
- ash
- rainforest
- **grow** (grow-grew-grown)

Gorillas live among the bamboo trees and nettles.

"Hungu and Kobwa, don't lag behind," Mama gorilla calls out.

"There may be poachers in the forest."

"We're coming," Kobwa answers.

She swings around a bamboo stalk.

The damp earth smells spicy from nettles.

Hungu grabs Kobwa from behind.

- bamboo
- nettle
- lag behind

- call out
- poacher
- **swing** (swing-swung-swung)

- stalk
- damp earth
- spicy

- grab

"Ha! I found you."

Kobwa squeals and scampers up the nearest tree.

"No fair, Hungu," Kobwa complains.

"I was talking to Mama, you hairy gorilla."

Kobwa sticks out her lip.

She crosses her arms on her chest.

She loves playing hide-and-seek with her brother.

He is fast, but she is smart.

KEY WORDS

- **find** (find-found-found)
- **squeal**
- **scamper**
- **nearest**
- **no fair**
- **complain**
- **hairy**
- **stick out one's lip** (stick-stuck-stuck)
- **cross arms**
- **play hide-and-seek**

Mountain gorillas are covered in black hair.

They have arms long enough to reach the ground. Aha!

Hungu grins and climbs his sister's tree.

"Someday, I'm going to be a hairy silverback gorilla," Hungu says.

The silverback is the leader of a gorilla family.

He is named for the gray hair on his back.

Kobwa pulls out of her brother's grasp.

"We had better go, Hungu," she says while glancing around quickly.

"Don't be such a coward," Hungu says.

KEY WORDS

- be covered in
- enough
- reach
- grin
- climb

- someday
- be going to
- silverback
- leader
- name for

- pull out of
- grasp
- had better
- glance
- coward

Hungu and Kobwa are twins.

Mountain gorilla twins are not common.

A set of twins is only born once every few years.

"I am serious, Hungu.

I can't see Mama and the family anymore," Kobwa says.

The forest is too thick.

The leaves hide the town below.

The trees block the six Virunga volcanoes.

The forest also hides the ten other members of the gorilla family.

"They are just through those trees.
Come on," Hungu says.
Hungu and Kobwa set off through the bamboo trees and nettles.

POP QUIZ

Mark T for true or F for false.

It is common that mountain gorillas have twins. T / F

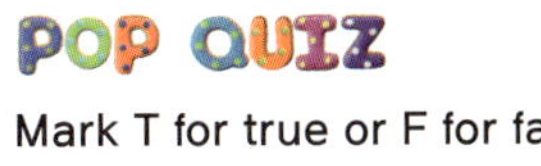

KEY WORDS

- twins
- common
- be born
- once
- serious
- can (= be able to)
- anymore
- thick
- leaf
- hide (hide-hid-hidden)
- below
- block
- through
- set off (set-set-set)

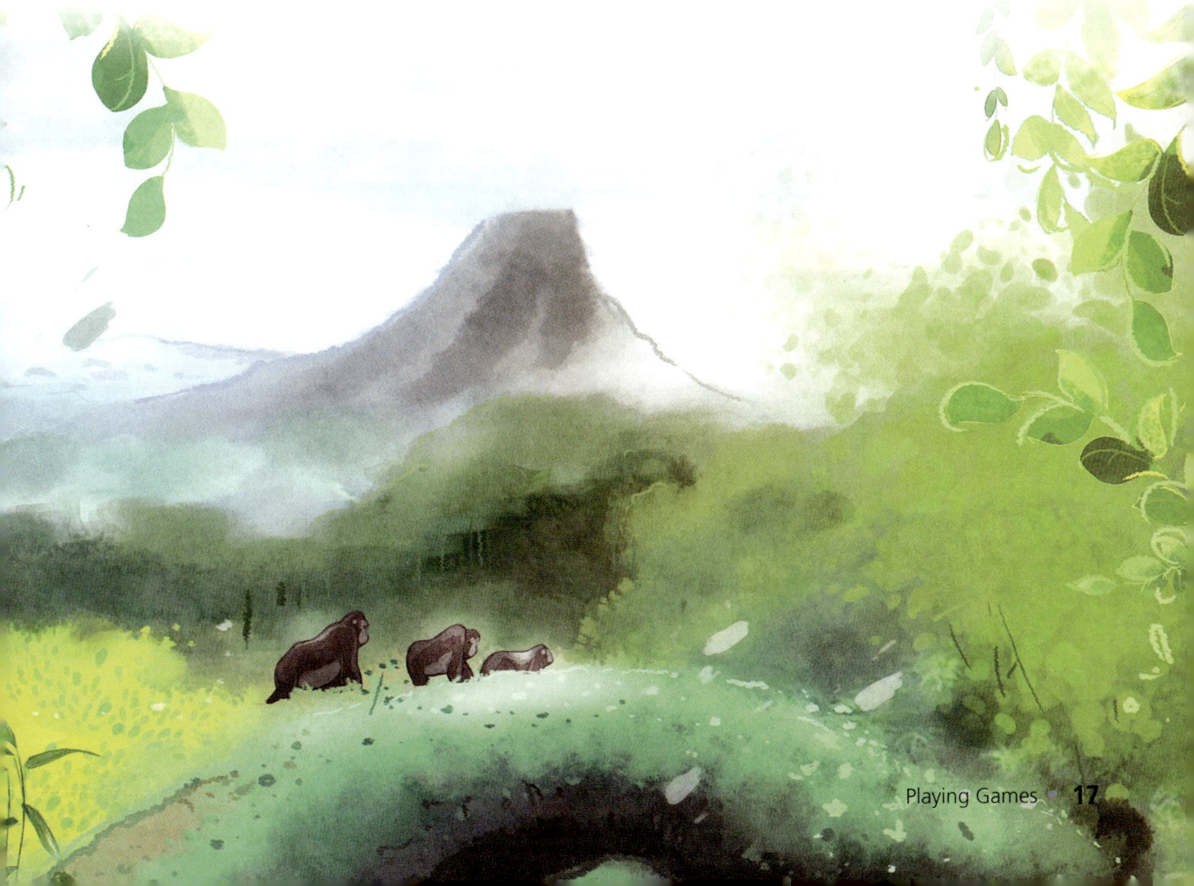

Bamboo is one of the fastest-growing plants in the world.

It is a member of the grass family.

Bamboo is tall and skinny like a column.

Nettles are short, shrubby plants.

The leaves and stems have stinging hairs.

They hurt humans, but not mountain gorillas.

There are also rosewood trees in the forest.

East African rosewood trees are massive and covered in moss.

They have reddish bark.

The wide canopy of leaves blocks the sun.

▲ nettle

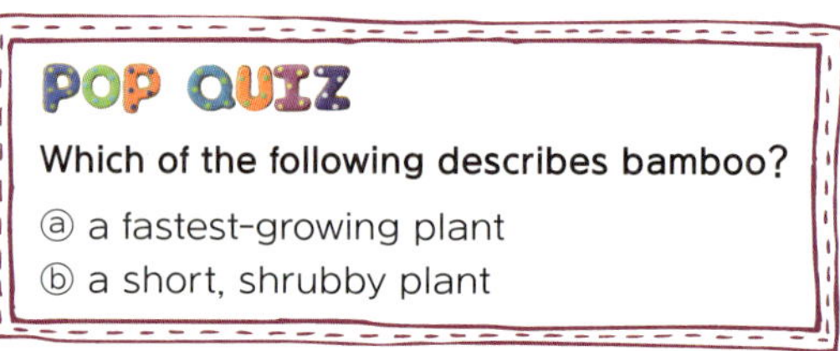

POP QUIZ

Which of the following describes bamboo?

ⓐ a fastest-growing plant
ⓑ a short, shrubby plant

KEY WORDS

- fastest
- grass family
- skinny
- column
- shrubby
- stem

- stinging
- stinging hair
- hurt (hurt-hurt-hurt)
- rosewood tree
- massive
- moss

- reddish
- bark
- wide
- canopy

Hungu and Kobwa follow some familiar gorilla signs.

Ripped nettles and leaves are scattered around. **Aha!**

Occasionally, they pass an old nest, too.

"I see something," Hungu says.

"Let's go."

A Fill in each blank with the right word below.

humans	arms	twins	ape

❶ The mountain gorilla is an endangered species of

______________.

❷ Mountain gorillas have ______________ long enough to reach

the ground.

❸ Hungu and Kobwa are ______________.

❹ Nettles hurt ______________, but not mountain gorillas.

B Mark T for true or F for false.

❶ The silverback is named for the gray hair on his legs.   T   F

❷ Mountain gorillas live among the bamboo trees and

nettles.   T   F

❸ A cloud forest is a colder type of rainforest.   T   F

❹ Bamboo is tall and fat.   T   F

C Choose the best answer to each question.

❶ Where is Rwanda?

a) in Central Africa

b) in Asia

c) in Europe

d) in South America

❷ What is NOT right about mountain gorillas?

a) Mountain gorillas live inside the Virunga volcanoes.

b) Mountain gorillas are covered in black hair.

c) Mountain gorilla twins are not common.

d) The silverback is the leader of the gorilla family.

D Put the sentences in order.

❶ Mama gorilla warned Hungu and Kobwa against a poacher.

❷ Hungu and Kobwa followed some familiar gorilla signs.

❸ Hungu grabbed Kobwa from behind.

❹ Hungu grinned and climbed his sister's tree.

_______ → _______ → _______ → _______

Chapter Two

Friends and Enemies

Hungu pushes through a stand of young bamboo trees.

Short and light green, they would be tasty.

A rustling in the trees above makes the gorillas glance up.

Hungu sees colorful feathers.

"Zuba, is that you?" he asks.

"Yes," Zuba answers.

He is a sunbird.

Zuba is mostly green.

He has a beige belly, a blue tail, and a red chest.

▲ sunbird

KEY WORDS

- enemy
- push through
- a stand of trees
- light green
- tasty
- rustling
- colorful
- feather
- sunbird
- mostly
- beige
- belly
- more than
- insect
- lately
- nectar
- as well
- flutter around
- land on
- nearby

More than a hundred species of birds live in the cloud forest.

"Found any good insects or spiders lately?" Hungu asks Zuba.

"Yes," Zuba says.

"I've had some lovely nectar as well."

Butterflies flutter around the gorillas.

"Ooh, pretty," Kobwa says.

A butterfly lands on a yellow flower nearby.

Hungu stares at the ground.

"What do you see, Hungu?" Kobwa asks.

He points.

"It's a chameleon. It has three horns."

"Is it about 30 centimeters long?" Zuba asks.

"Yes."

"It is a three-horned chameleon," Zuba says.

"They keep me company sometimes."

Kobwa takes a few steps away.

"Here is a termite mound."

▲ three-horned chameleon

▲ termite mound

KEY WORDS

- stare at
- point
- three-horned chameleon

- keep ~ company (keep-kept-kept)
- take a step (take-took-taken)
- termite mound

"It's why I'm in this tree," Zuba says.

"Termites are tasty."

"Yes, I like a good termite sometimes, too,"

Hungu says.

"Other insects are tasty as well.

But we mostly eat plants."

"Enjoy your lunch, Zuba," Kobwa says.

"We had better go.

We need to find our family."

"Be careful, my friends," Zuba warns.

"I saw an African golden cat yesterday." Aha!

Kobwa gasps.

"They are rare. No one has seen one here in years."

"They are fierce hunters," Hungu says.

"Sometimes they even hunt small mountain gorillas," Kobwa says.

Hungu bumps into his sister.

"Don't worry, Kobwa. I'll keep you safe."

Kobwa doesn't feel safe.

"African golden cats are between 61 and 102 centimeters long.

They weigh between 3 and 18 kilograms," Kobwa says.

▲ African golden cat

- careful
- gasp
- rare
- fierce
- hunter
- hunt
- bump into
- keep
- between
- weigh

"They aren't heavy compared to an adult gorilla,"
Hungu says.

"True, but we aren't adults," Kobwa says.

"At least there are no more leopards
here," Zuba says.

"Leopards climb trees," Hungu
says.

"African golden cats climb trees,
too," Kobwa adds.

Zuba twitters a song.

"They can't fly. Don't worry about
me."

▲ leopard

POP QUIZ

What animal do African golden cats
sometimes hunt?

ⓐ leopards
ⓑ small mountain gorillas

KEY WORDS

- compare
- adult
- at least
- no more
- leopard
- add
- twitter
- worry

Suddenly, the usual forest sounds stop.

Zuba stands still and listens. The butterflies leave.

The chameleon changes color and disappears under some leaves.

"What is happening?" Hungu asks.

"Something is coming," Kobwa says.

"I think it's an African golden cat," Zuba says.

"Run, my friends!"

Zuba flies away. Hungu and Kobwa turn away.

A reddish-brown animal moves toward them.

It is a kind of cat.

This cat has white spots above its eyes.

The fur around its ears is dark brown.

The tip of its tail is black. Its neck is white.

"Kobwa?" Hungu asks.

"Yes?"

"Is that an African golden cat?" he asks.

"Yes."

They take small steps backward.

They move very slowly.

"What should we do?" Hungu asks.

"I don't know," Kobwa says.

"He is big for a cat," Hungu says. Aha!

"Yes," Kobwa answers.

"He has a long tail, too," Hungu says.

Kobwa nods slowly.

They take another slow step.

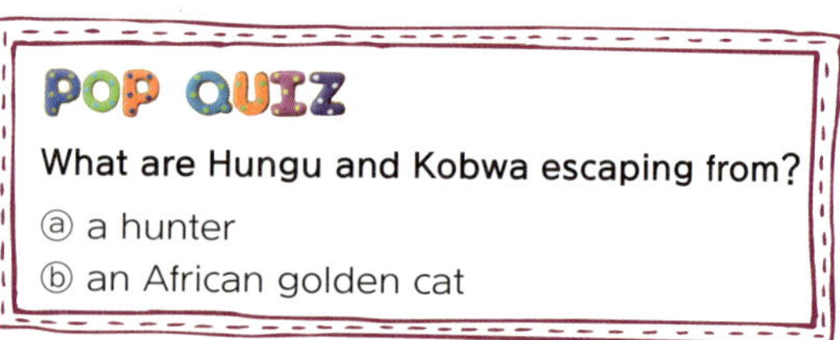

KEY WORDS

- take steps backward
- should (= have to)
- nod
- how to + *Verb*
- escape

The African golden cat stares.

"Should we run?" Hungu asks.

"African golden cats are fast," Kobwa says.

"Should we climb a tree?" Hungu asks.

"African golden cats climb trees," Kobwa says.

Kobwa thinks about how to escape.

She thinks about what gorillas can do.

"They climb trees, but they don't swing," Kobwa says.

"We can swing from branch to branch.

This is how we can get away."

They each back up against a tree.

"On the count of three," Hungu says.

"One, two, three. Climb!"

They jump for a branch.

They climb quickly up the tree.

"Now, swing," Hungu yells.

Hungu swings off a branch into a nearby tree.

Kobwa does the same.

They swing one more time.

Hungu looks behind him.

KEY WORDS

- branch to branch
- get away (get-got-gotten)
- each
- back up
- against

- on the count of three
- yell
- off
- one more time
- look behind

The African golden cat sits in its original tree.

It reaches a paw for a branch.

"It wants to try swinging," Hungu says.

They watch the cat.

It misses the branch and falls to the ground.

It walks away.

Kobwa sighs with relief.

"Keep swinging, Kobwa," Hungu says.

"Let's get farther away."

They swing through a few more trees.

Then, they jump to the ground.

- original
- paw
- try
- miss
- **fall** (fall-fell-fallen)
- walk away
- sigh with relief
- keep + *Verb*-ing
- get farther away
- scary
- great idea
- save
- **shake one's head** (shake-shook-shaken)
- realize

"That was scary," Kobwa says.

"You had a great idea," Hungu says.

"You saved us from the cat."

Kobwa shakes her head.

"Yes, Kobwa. You are smart.

You realized gorillas can swing, but cats can't."

"Okay, let's find Mama," Kobwa says.

A Match each animal with its feature correctly.

❶   •   • a) It can change its color.

❷   •   • b) It has colorful feathers and eats insects.

❸   •   • c) It weighs between 3 and 18 kilograms.

B Mark T for true or F for false.

❶ African golden cats hunt adult mountain gorillas.   T   F

❷ Mountain gorillas eat plants.   T   F

❸ Zuba is an enemy of Hungu and Kobwa.   T   F

❹ More than a hundred different species of birds live in the cloud forest.   T   F

Choose the best answer to each question.

❶ What is NOT right about African golden cats?

a) African golden cats are rare.

b) African golden cats have a long tail.

c) African golden cats weigh less than an adult mountain gorilla.

d) African golden cats can swing from branches to branches.

❷ What can African golden cats do?

a) climbing trees　　　　　b) digging

c) flying　　　　　　　　d) swimming

❸ What is NOT sunbird food?

a) spider　　　　　　　　b) termite

c) nectar　　　　　　　　d) leopard

❹ What is NOT right about animals living in a cloud forest?

a) Leopards climb trees.

b) African golden cats are fierce hunters for small mountain
gorillas.

c) Mountain gorillas mostly eat meat.

d) Three-horned chameleons are about 30 centimeters long.

Tourists

Hungu and Kobwa set off again through the cloud forest.

"I hear something," Hungu says while cocking his head toward the sound.

A twig cracks.

The gorillas hear murmurs.

"Let's go this way," Hungu says.

Kobwa puts her hand on her brother's arm.

"No, wait, Hungu. Those aren't gorilla sounds."

"Then let's see what it is," Hungu says.

He steps around a tree and through branches.

"No, Hungu, wait."

KEY WORDS

- tourist
- cock one's head
- twig
- crack
- murmur
- put hand on (put-put-put)
- step around

Hungu freezes, his hands on the ground.

The murmur grows louder.

Kobwa slowly approaches her brother.

She peers over his shoulder.

Then, she relaxes.

Staring at Hungu is a circle of humans.

They wear smiles and rain slickers.

They carry cameras. They do not point guns.

KEY WORDS

- **freeze** (freeze-froze-frozen)
- **approach**
- **peer**
- **over**
- **relax**
- **a circle of humans**
- **wear a smile** (wear-wore-worn)
- **slicker**
- **carry**
- **point a gun**

Tourists! **Aha!**

Kobwa jumps around.

She grunts with pleasure.

Tourists are fun.

Hungu starts to move closer to the tourists.

"No, Hungu," Kobwa says.

"It isn't safe to get close to them.

Mama told us they can make us sick."

"Relax, Kobwa.

No one is coughing or sneezing," Hungu says.

Kobwa warns.

"Be careful, Hungu.

Humans can still be dangerous to us."

The humans smile, laugh, and snap pictures of the two young gorillas.

A man with dark skin and wearing khaki pants and a
khaki vest is their guide.

"These are young mountain gorillas," the guide says.

"Notice their thick fur.

The cloud forest is chilly.

Their fur keeps them warm.

The forest is especially cold at night."

Hungu rubs his hands over his hairy arms.

"It does get cold at night," Hungu says.

"Someday, these gorillas may grow as tall as two meters," the guide says. 

"They will weigh as much as 160 kilograms."

The group of tourists snaps more pictures.

> ## POP QUIZ
>
> **Who is the person explaining mountain gorillas to tourists?**
>
> ⓐ a soldier
> ⓑ a guide

KEY WORDS

- skin
- khaki
- guide
- notice
- chilly
- keep warm
- rub someone's hand
- get cold

"Gorilla families are very stable," the Rwandan guide says.

"They can have up to fifty animals.

Usually, there are only ten or so.

These two must have wandered off."

"We are playing hide-and-seek," Hungu explains.

"Mountain gorillas travel between one and two kilometers per day.

They eat while they walk.

I wonder how far these two have traveled," the guide says.

"It didn't seem very far," Hungu says.

"Kobwa, I don't think they can hear us."

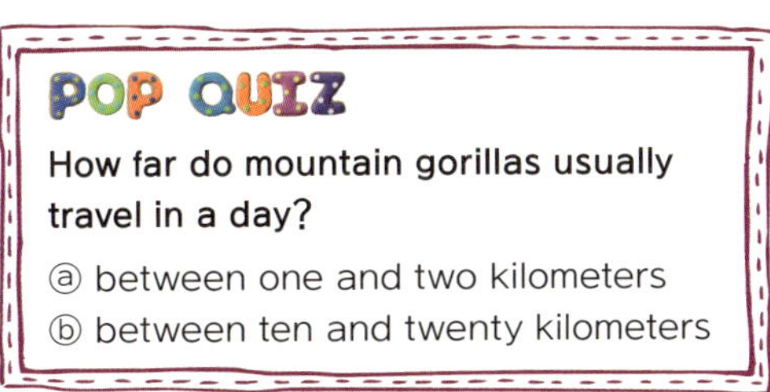

KEY WORDS

- stable
- Rwandan
- up to
- usually
- wander off
- explain
- travel
- per day
- wonder
- seem

Kobwa laughs.

"They hear you. They just don't speak gorilla language."

"Remember, everyone, if we come across the silverback, be very humble," the guide continues. 

"Don't make him angry. Do not make eye contact. He is the defender of the family. He will roar and beat his chest. The silverback might charge if he finds you threatening."

▲ silverback

"I thought gorillas were very tolerant of people,"
a tourist says.

She has white skin and blond hair.

"Yes, they are. Just don't look him in the eye.

Move slowly and carefully.

Don't give him any reason

to get mad," the guide

explains.

"If the silverback comes,

the family will be with

him," Hungu says.

Kobwa nods.

▲ gorilla family

POP QUIZ

Choose the right word for the underlined part.

The silverback is the defender of the
(ⓐ forest / ⓑ family).

KEY WORDS

- **speak** (speak-spoke-spoken)
- remember
- come across
- humble
- continue
- make eye contact
- defender
- roar
- beat
- charge
- threatening
- tolerant
- blond
- look someone in the eye
- reason
- get mad

"Gorillas are closely related to humans," the guide says.

"Their genetic code is similar to ours.  And they share some of our behavior."

"I love watching humans," Hungu says.

He hugs his sister.

"See?" the guide asks.

"They hug and play like we do."

Hungu and Kobwa laugh.

"Have you noticed their hands?" the guide asks.

"They have a thumb plus four other fingers. Like us."

▲ a playful gorilla

▲ A gorilla's hand is similar to a human's.

KEY WORDS

- be closely related to
- genetic code
- similar
- share
- behavior
- hug
- thumb

"Aren't they the apes most in danger?" another tourist
asks.

This one has short black hair and round eyeglasses.

"Yes," the guide says.

"Only a few hundred mountain gorillas remain around
the Virunga volcanoes."

"Is that a lot?" Hungu asks Kobwa.

She shakes her head.

"Mama says we used to have more family. **Aha!**
They used to cross the borders freely."

"The gorillas are losing their forests to farmland and
fuel," the guide explains.

KEY WORDS

- remain
- cross
- border
- freely
- farmland
- fuel

- require
- clear of
- cut down (cut-cut-cut)
- firewood
- charcoal
- little by little

"People need more land for farming.
Farming requires land cleared of trees.
They also cut down trees to use as firewood and to make charcoal."
"Is that true, Kobwa?" Hungu asks his sister.
"Are we losing our home?"
Kobwa nods.
"Little by little, people are cutting down our forest."

"The wars here have also made gorilla habitat smaller
and less safe," the guide says.
"What about poaching?" another tourist asks.
"Isn't there illegal hunting of mountain gorillas?"
The guide nods his head sadly.

KEY WORDS

- habitat
- less
- poach
- illegal (↔ legal)
- sadly
- government
- pass a law against
- roam
- armed guard
- army uniform

"Yes, the government passed laws against poaching.
However, hunters continue to roam these forests.
This is why we have armed guards."
He nods toward two young men in army uniforms.

"Hungu, Mama saw poachers here a few days ago.

We had better return to the family," Kobwa says.

Hungu nods.

"You're right.

We have been gone a long time.

Mama and the others are probably worried."

Hungu grunts a goodbye to the tourists.

He makes a new path through the bamboo trees.

Kobwa follows close behind.

"I hope we find the family soon," Kobwa says.

"I'm getting scared."

"Don't worry, sister. I'm here," Hungu says, puffing out his chest.

POP QUIZ

What did Hungu do to find his family?

ⓐ He followed Kobwa.
ⓑ He made a new path through the bamboo trees.

KEY WORDS

- a few days ago
- return
- gone
- probably
- worried
- make a path
- close behind
- get scared
- puff out one's chest

Comprehension Quiz

A Mark T for true or F for false.

❶ It is safe for gorillas to get close to humans.   T   F

❷ Tourists should always make eye contact with the silverback.   T   F

❸ The gorilla's genetic code is similar to that of humans.   T   F

❹ Despite laws against poaching, hunters continue to roam the forests.   T   F

B Circle the right word(s) for each underlined part.

❶ Humans can make gorillas (cry / sick).

❷ Poaching is the illegal (cooking / hunting) of animals.

❸ When the silverback is angry, he will (roar / sleep) and beat his chest.

❹ Someday, Hungu and Kobwa may grow as tall as (two meters / five meters).

 Choose the best answer to each question.

❶ How much does an adult gorilla weigh?

a) 100 grams

b) 160 grams

c) 60 kilograms

d) 160 kilograms

❷ How many fingers does a gorilla have in one hand?

a) 2   b) 3

c) 4   d) 5

❸ What is NOT right about mountain gorillas?

a) Mountain gorilla families are very stable.

b) Mountain gorillas travel between one and two kilometers per day.

c) Mountain gorillas are the most common apes.

d) Mountain gorillas are very tolerant of people.

Chapter Four

Poacher

Hungu picks up the pace through the trees.

Kobwa can barely keep up with her brother.

Soon, he nearly collides with a human.

The man has dark skin, rough black hair, khaki pants, and boots.

He looks very much like the guide they left behind with the tourists.

The tourists smiled.

They enjoyed the gorillas.

This man, however, does not smile. 

Hungu freezes.

POP QUIZ

Whom does the man that Hungu and Kobwa meet look similar to?

ⓐ the guide
ⓑ one of the tourists

KEY WORDS

- pick up the pace
- barely
- keep up with
- nearly

- collide with
- rough
- leave behind

Kobwa holds onto her brother.

She peers over his shoulders.

The man is a poacher!

Their mother warned them.

Instead of listening to her, they kept playing hide-and-seek.

They lost their family in the thick woods.

Hunters kill gorillas as trophies and for their fur.

Hungu and Kobwa have to get away. Aha!

The man points something long, thin, and shiny at Hungu's hairy chest.

"It's a rifle," Kobwa says.

"He can't get us both unless we stand here," Hungu grunts.

"Do you remember the giant tree that just started to bloom?"

"Y-y-yes, but…" Kobwa stammers.

How will flowers help them?

"I'll meet you there," Hungu says.

"Run!"

- **hold onto** (hold-held-held)
- **instead of**
- **lose** (lose-lost-lost)
- **thick woods**

- trophy
- rifle
- both
- unless

- giant
- bloom
- stammer

Hungu dives under the man's raised arm.

He runs into the dark forest.

Kobwa climbs the nearest tree.

She leaps off a branch into the farthest tree she can reach.

She keeps swinging from tree to tree.

Soon, she can no longer hear the man crashing through the leaves below her.

Kobwa lands silently on the soft ground.

She looks all around her.

The air is spicy from the nettles under her feet.

She stands under the tree's spiny leaves.

She picks at her fur.

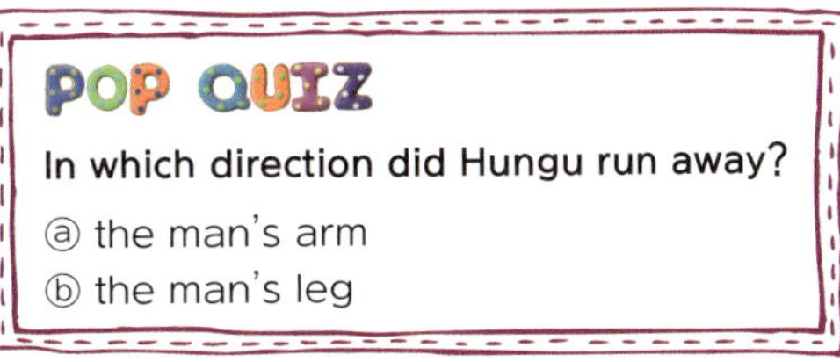

KEY WORDS

- dive
- raised
- run into (run-ran-run)
- leap off
- farthest
- from A to B

- no longer
- crash through
- silently (= quietly)
- spiny
- pick at

Where is Hungu?

Kobwa hopes the poacher didn't catch her brother.

Her eyes open wide in fright.

She will never forgive herself for playing hide-and-seek.

They should have stayed with their mother. **Aha!**

Despite her worry and impatience, she grabs some thistle leaves to eat.

Gorillas eat a lot.

They eat all day.

A thud makes Kobwa whip her head around.

"Hungu!" she cries.

"You made it."

Her face is as expressive as a human's.

Hungu shakes his head to dislodge a few clinging leaves.

"Here I am. The poacher is not far behind. Let's go."

Holding Kobwa's hand, Hungu leads her past piles of
dried leaves.

- open wide
- in fright
- never
- **forgive** (forgive-forgave-forgiven)
- despite
- impatience
- thistle

- thud
- whip around
- expressive
- dislodge
- clinging
- **lead** (lead-led-led)
- a pile of

Twigs crack with each step.

"Those nests are too old," Hungu says.

"We have to find fresh ones if we're going to find the family."

"No, Hungu."

Kobwa shakes her head at her brother.

"They will take us in the wrong direction."

She frowns while thinking.

"We slept in the newest nests last night.

Going toward the newest nests means going back the way we came," she says.

"The family isn't going backward."

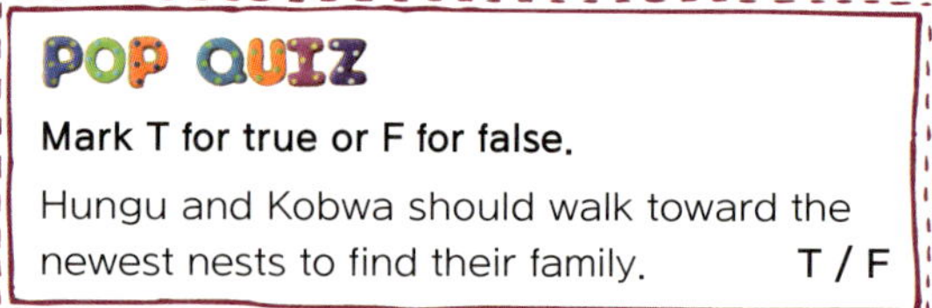

KEY WORDS

- fresh
- direction
- frown
- newest
- mean (mean-meant-meant)
- go backward (go-went-gone)
- munch
- forehead
- wrinkle
- in thought
- rising

Hungu munches on a nettle and looks at his sister.

His forehead wrinkles in thought.

"You're right, Kobwa.

How do we find them?"

Hungu asks.

"This morning, the silverback started walking in the direction of the rising sun," Kobwa explains.

"That's the direction we need to walk in now."

Hungu nods.

"You lead."

"No, I c-c-can't," Kobwa answers.

She pulls away from her brother.

"What if I lead us s-s-straight to the p-p-poacher?
Or, or…"

"You won't. You're so smart."

Hungu gives Kobwa a nettle to chew.

She chews and stares at her brother.

"Come on. We don't want the man to catch up to us,"
he says.

"Maybe he will follow us to the family.
The silverback will take care of him."

The silverback will attack any human who threatens the family.

"Maybe we will find another group of tourists," Hungu says.

"The soldiers won't let the poacher hurt us.
They have guns, too."

Kobwa takes the leaf and her brother's hand.

"Okay, this way."

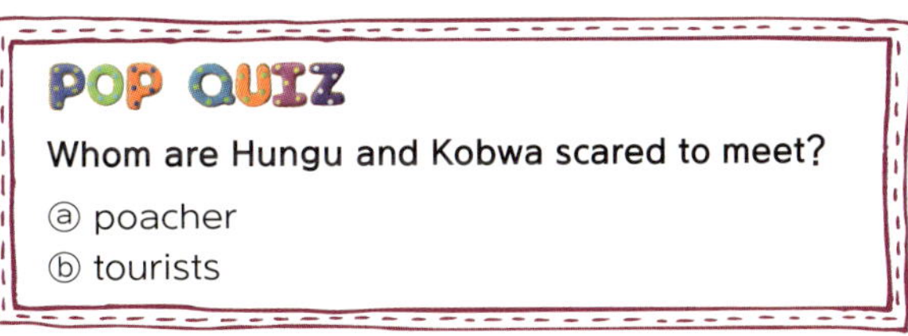

KEY WORDS

- pull away from
- straight
- chew
- catch up to (catch-caught-caught)
- maybe

- take care of
- attack
- threaten
- soldier
- let

Hungu and Kobwa walk under umbrella-like trees.

The air around them cools.

Birds shriek less frequently.

Kobwa hopes their family is safe.

"Climb this tree, Hungu.

Tell me if you see anything ahead."

Hungu scrambles nimbly up the tree.

He looks in the direction

Kobwa indicates.

"I see Mama!" Hungu shouts.

Then, he loses his footing and falls onto the damp nettles.

He lands in front of Kobwa.

"Mama is in a tree up ahead," he says.

"I think I smell the silverback now," Kobwa says.

Silverback gorillas have a strong scent.

The odor lets other family members know where he is.

KEY WORDS

- cool
- shriek
- frequently
- ahead
- scramble
- nimbly
- indicate
- shout
- lose one's footing
- in front of
- have a strong scent
- odor

The brother and sister run and run.

They swing from tree to tree.

They fall breathlessly into the arms of their waiting family.

"We're so glad you two are all right," their mother says.

"Kobwa, why do you look so scared?"

Kobwa's round eyes widen.

She hugs her mother tightly.

"We ran into a poacher.

We had to run away."

Hungu tells the story.

He ends by saying, "Kobwa was amazing.

She knew how to find you."

POP QUIZ

What does Kobwa do when she meets Mom?

ⓐ She hugs her mother tightly.
ⓑ She grabs some thistle leaves.

KEY WORDS

- breathlessly
- all right
- widen
- tightly
- run away
- end

"You both have done very well," the silverback gorilla says.

"You outsmarted and outran the poacher.

Someday, you both will lead this family well."

Hungu smiles shyly at his sister.

Kobwa knows it is his dream to lead the family as a silverback. **Aha!**

She reaches out and grabs him around the middle.

"Now I've got you!" she yells.

KEY WORDS

- outsmart
- outrun (outrun-outran-outrun)
- shyly
- as
- reach out
- middle

A Who said what? Match each line with the right character.

❶ 
Kobwa

❷ 
Hungu

❸ 
Silverback

a) "You both have done very well."

b) "You're so smart."

c) "Going toward the newest nests means going back the way we came."

B Circle the right word(s) for each underlined part.

❶ Kobwa's face is as expressive as a (human's / sunbird's).

❷ Hungu sees his mama when he climbs a (tree / volcano).

❸ The silverback's odor let the other family members know (that he is angry / where he is).

❹ The silverback is (afraid of / proud of) Kobwa and Hungu.

C Choose the correct word for each blank.

❶ The poacher has a ______________.

    a) rifle　　　　　　　　b) hat

    c) raincoat　　　　　　　d) sword

❷ Hunters kill gorillas for their ______________.

    a) bamboo　　　　　　　b) fur

    c) nests　　　　　　　　d) tails

❸ Silverback gorillas have a strong ______________.

    a) nest　　　　　　　　b) scent

    c) tree　　　　　　　　d) gun

D Mark T for true or F for false.

❶ Hunters kill gorillas as trophies.　　　　　　　　　T　F

❷ Hungu and Kobwa should find the newest nests to find the family.　　　　　T　F

❸ Hungu and Kobwa walk in the direction of the rising sun.　　　　　T　F

❹ Hungu and Kobwa couldn't find their family in the end.　　T　F

Let's Review the Story

Fill in the blanks to review the story.

Title: Hide-and-Seek Gorillas

Place: In the cloud forest

Event: Two __________ lose their family.

Chapter 1:

• The mountain gorilla is an endangered species of __________.

• The silverback is the l__________ of the gorilla family.

• The forest is filled with b__________, nettles, and rosewood trees.

Chapter 2:

• Zuba is a colorful __________.

• Gorillas mostly eat p__________.

• African golden cats are fierce __________ but are rare.

Chapter 3:

• Humans can be __________ to mountain gorillas.

• Gorillas have thick __________ to keep them warm.

• Gorillas are closely related to h__________.

Chapter 4:

• Hunters kill gorillas for their __________ and as trophies.

• A gorilla's face is as __________ as a human's.

• The silverback will __________ any human who threatens the family.

Let's Think & Talk

Think about the following questions and answer them freely.

❶ What characteristics of mountain gorillas are similar to humans?

❷ If you were Hungu and Kobwa, how would you do to escape from the poacher?

❸ Tell us what you learned for the first time about mountain gorillas through the book.

❹ Humans are not only mountain gorillas' friends, but also their enemies. Explain the reason. Then tell us why we should protect mountain gorillas and how you think we can protect them.

Let's Review the Story

Title: Hide-and-Seek Gorillas

Place: In the cloud forest

Event: Two mountain gorillas lose their family.

Chapter 1:

- The mountain gorilla is an endangered species of ape .
- The silverback is the leader of the gorilla family.
- The forest is filled with bamboo , nettles, and rosewood trees.

Chapter 2:

- Zuba is a colorful sunbird .
- Gorillas mostly eat plants .
- African golden cats are fierce hunters but are rare.

Chapter 3:

- Humans can be dangerous to mountain gorillas.
- Gorillas have thick fur to keep them warm.
- Gorillas are closely related to humans .

Chapter 4:

- Hunters kill gorillas for their fur and as trophies.
- A gorilla's face is as expressive as a human's.
- The silverback will attack any human who threatens the family.

Smart Readers: **Wise** & **Wide**

After-reading **Test**

- Hide-and-Seek Gorillas

- Level 3

- 25 Questions

  (Vocabulary 4 / Reading Comprehension 16 /

  Sentence Structure & Grammar 5)

1. Which of the following is similar to the word "silently"?

    Kobwa lands silently on the soft ground.

    ① nimbly
    ② quietly
    ③ frequently
    ④ shyly

2. Which pair has the wrong past tense form of the listed verb?

    ① hide – hidden   ② set – set
    ③ swing – swung   ④ fall – fell

3. Which of the following does NOT have the similar meaning with the word "swing"?

    ① scamper   ② scramble
    ③ dive   ④ outsmart

4. Which of the following is similar to the word "peer"?

    ① freeze   ② grunt
    ③ stare   ④ gasp

5. Which of the following places is NOT related to a mountain gorilla's habitat?

    ① Rwanda   ② slopes of Virunga volcanoes
    ③ South Korea   ④ cloud forest

6. Which of the following is NOT mountain gorilla food?
   ① thistle leaves   ② nettle
   ③ termite   ④ sunbird

7. What is NOT right about mountain gorillas?
   ① Mountain gorillas are covered in black hair.
   ② The silverback is the leader of the gorilla family.
   ③ Thousands of mountain gorillas remain around the Virunga volcanoes.
   ④ Mountain gorilla twins are only born once every few years.

8. What are Hungu and Kobwa afraid of?
   ① sunbird
   ② three-horned chameleon
   ③ African golden cat
   ④ small mountain gorilla

9. What is NOT right about an African golden cat?
   ① The African golden cat is slow.
   ② The African golden cat is between 61 and 102 centimeters long.
   ③ The African golden cat can climb trees.
   ④ The African golden cat has a long tail.

10. Why is Kobwa afraid of tourists?
   ① The tourists can make mountain gorillas sick.
   ② The tourists snapped pictures.
   ③ Kobwa saw a man holding a gun.
   ④ Zuba warned Kobwa against tourists.

11. What characteristic of mountain gorillas is NOT similar to humans?

① Mountain gorillas' genetic code is similar to that of humans.
② Mountain gorillas and humans have a thumb plus four other fingers.
③ Mountain gorillas and humans can hug and play.
④ Mountain gorillas and humans are the apes most in danger.

12. What is NOT the cause of the mountain gorillas' habitat loss?

① cutting down the forest for farming and fuel
② taking many pictures
③ illegal hunting
④ the wars

13. What is right about a silverback and the gorilla family that he leads?

① A gorilla family can have up to 5 animals.
② The silverback might charge if he finds any human threatening.
③ The silverback is the baby of the family.
④ The silverback will roar and beat his chest when he gets tired.

14. What is NOT a characteristic of the poacher whom Hungu and Kobwa meet?

① His black hair is rough.
② He wears khaki pants and boots.
③ He does not smile.
④ He wears rain slicker.

15. What did the poacher aim at when he tried to kill Hungu and Kobwa?

① a camera   ② a rifle
③ a trap   ④ thistles

16. What did Hungu and Kobwa do to escape from the poacher?
    ① running and swinging
    ② climbing and swimming
    ③ walking and crawling
    ④ shouting and beating

17. What helped Hungu and Kobwa to find their family?
    ① the odor of nettles
    ② other gorillas
    ③ the strong scent of the silverback
    ④ a poacher

18. What is Hungu's dream?
    ① to lead the family as a silverback
    ② to hunt African golden cats
    ③ to live with people
    ④ to make the war stop

※ Choose the correct word or phrase for each blank. (19~20)

19. Mountain gorillas live among the bamboo trees and ____________.

    ① rainforest   ② potato fields
    ③ pine trees   ④ nettles

20. Mountain gorillas can ____________, but the African golden cats can't.

    ① hunt   ② swing
    ③ climb   ④ swim

21. Choose the correct sentence.

    ① Kobwa thinks about how to escaped.

    ② Kobwa thinks about how to be escaped.

    ③ Kobwa thinks about how to escape.

    ④ Kobwa thinks about how escape.

※ Choose the wrong part of the sentence. (22~25)

22.
Mama <u>says</u> we <u>used to</u> <u>having</u> more <u>family</u>.
     ①   ②   ③   ④

23.
They <u>should have</u> <u>staying</u> <u>with</u> <u>their mother</u>.
    ①   ② ③   ④

24.
<u>Hungu and Kobwa</u> have <u>to</u> <u>getting</u> <u>away</u>.
    ①   ② ③   ④

25.
Kobwa <u>knows</u> <u>what</u> is his dream <u>to lead</u> the family <u>as</u> a silverback.
    ①   ②   ③   ④

Brooke Rousseau

Brooke Rousseau is a writer, mother, and French teacher who strives to make the exotic familiar. Driven by a fascination with other cultures, Brooke has lived in Europe, Africa, and the United States, and visited parts of the Middle East and South America. She has earned degrees in French Literature and International Relations. Brooke writes nonfiction for older elementary children, short stories for very young children, and middle grade and young adult novels.

Hide-and-Seek Gorillas

Written by Brooke Rousseau
Illustrated by Yeseon Cho

First Published in May 2015

Editorial Manager: Juyon Choi
Editors: Jiyeong Park, Kyunghee Jang
Designers: Eunhee Lee, Elim
Cover Designer: Eunhee Lee

Published and distributed by

Darakwon Bldg., 64-1 Jandari-ro, Mapo-gu, Seoul, Korea 121-894
Tel: 82-2-736-2031(ext. 250)   Fax: 82-2-732-2037
Homepage: www.ihappyhouse.co.kr
Publisher: Kyudo Chung

ISBN: 978-89-6653-192-9 18740 / 978-89-6653-156-1 18740(set)

[Components]
• 1 Audio CD (Recording Studio: Aram)
• Answer Keys & Korean Translation: Free download at www.ihappyhouse.co.kr